BRING THE OUTDOORS IN

BRING THE OUTDOORS IN

Garden Projects for Decorating
and Styling Your Home

SHANE POWERS

WITH JENNIFER CEGIELSKI

Photographs by Gentl & Hyers

CHRONICLE BOOKS
SAN FRANCISCO

Library of Congress Cataloging-in-Publication Data

Powers, Shane.
  Bring the outdoors in : garden projects for decorating and styling your home /
Shane Powers with Jennifer Cegielski ; photographs by Gentl & Hyers.
       p. cm.
  ISBN 978-1-4521-0754-7
  1. Floral decorations. 2. Flower arrangement—Pictorial works. 3. Garden
ornaments and furniture. 4. Handicraft. I. Cegielski, Jennifer. II. Title.
  SB449.P67 2013
  745.92—dc23
                        2012013904

Manufactured in China

Designed by Allison Weiner

10 9 8 7 6 5 4 3 2 1

Chronicle Books LLC
680 Second Street
San Francisco, California 94107
www.chroniclebooks.com

FSC
www.fsc.org
MIX
Paper from
responsible sources
FSC® C008047

CONTENTS

INTRODUCTION

I've been fascinated by the natural world for as long as I can remember. I didn't start working with botanicals though until I got a job as a photo stylist for the groundbreaking publication *Bloom*. The founder, Li Edelkoort, encouraged me to think beyond traditional uses, and focus instead on plants and flowers as more dynamic elements. I began to look at their shapes, colors, and textures with a new perspective.

My work grew to include art directing and styling interiors and still lifes for other magazines such as *Vogue Living Australia* and *Blueprint*, and often I brought living things into the mix. A crafter at heart, I honed my skills as an editor of craft assignments (many of which included plants and flowers) for the incredible team at *Martha Stewart Living*. Eventually, these opportunities led to the development of my indoor garden collection for West Elm. For this collaboration we created simple, contemporary solutions for some of my favorite botanicals—air plants, water plants, cut flowers, and dried elements. Researching and sketching my ideas was a great exercise and the result is a collection of versatility. All of these experiences—styling, decorating, using plant materials, crafting, developing products—have influenced my approach to the projects found in these pages.

While I've had the good fortune to work with designers and artisans all over the world, it's also true that there is no place like home. For my own home, I look for specimens that common wisdom might say belong outside—mosses, vines, aquatic plants, ferns—and bring them in to create moments of natural and unexpected beauty. These displays might happen anywhere indoors, perhaps as a garland of *Tillandsia* hanging in the corner of a room or in a landscape of ivy cuttings trailing along a shelf, or even in more surprising ways like artwork made using natural elements. For plantings, I fully consider the container and supporting materials along with the main botanical focus so that the entire presentation—from the hook to the plant to the pot—works together to become an incredible object. Sentimental as it sounds, it's rewarding to watch something grow and flourish under the care of your own hand in the rooms where you live. And aesthetically speaking, bringing a bit of the natural world indoors introduces unusual colors and textures that enhance our interiors and balance the hard lines of our furnishings.

While trends in flowers and gardening may come and go, the ideas in this book have a timeless appeal to be enjoyed and referenced for years to come. The projects are not gardening projects per se; they are three-dimensional still lifes, miniature worlds designed to enhance your interiors. Some are created with living plants while others use dried materials. The collection includes cut arrangements, potted landscapes, single planters, tableaus of multiples, hanging and water gardens, pressed assemblages, and topiary and terrarium-style projects. At the back, I've included a list of sources to help get you started with supplies. Most of the projects are made with easy-to-find materials and require minimal maintenance. Even if you don't consider yourself a green thumb you will find something here to create. Remember that the organic process is an irregular one. Your own versions of these projects might not turn out exactly like those in the pictures and they will evolve in their own way, but that is the amazing and wild beauty of nature.

GETTING STARTED

The overall process of bringing the natural world into your home isn't diffi-cult—at its core it's about choosing the right botanical element to fit with the style of your space and the right location for your plants to flourish. To help you get started, here are some basic care tips to help you determine the best botanicals for your interior, as well as tips for choosing contain-ers and supporting materials, and a list of important tools.

LOCATION, LIGHT & TEMPERATURE First, take a good look around your home and assess what you see. What areas could use a touch of nature? Or, if you are inspired by a particular idea in these pages, have a look around your home to find the best place for it. The small scale of these projects means that they'll work in a variety of locations—tabletops, mantels, shelves, windowsills, bookcases, and even hanging from doorknobs or suspended from the ceiling. Think about the rooms where you spend a lot of time, as well as unexpected spots that could benefit from a little romance, like the stairs at an entryway.

When picking a location, consider the light and temperature. You need to be sure that a plant will survive in the spot you choose. Ask yourself: Does this room get enough light? Does it get too much light? Is it too warm, too cool, too dry? Are there air-conditioning or heating vents nearby that could dramatically alter the temperature? Is there a window that will let in too much cold or hot air? Most of the live plants in these projects flourish in partial shade and indirect light indoors, but certain plant groups have very specific needs. Succulents, for example, require full southern sun exposure to thrive, while *Tillandsias* (air plants) need bright but indirect light. From a climate perspective, ferns and mosses require considerable humidity. The list of plant types below should act as a general guide to the conditions and care required for the plants in these projects. Live plants are usually sold with care instructions; be sure to follow these instructions for optimal results.

PLANT TYPES You may be drawn to a particular project because you find the plant appealing for its color, texture, or shape, whether it's something soft and lush like moss or something striking and geometric like succulents. You might choose to work with a single plant or several in a similar variety, or even an assortment of different types of plants. Beyond living plants, you might wish to arrange fresh-cut vines or flowers or create more lasting arrangements from dried flowers and plants or pressed cuttings. Whichever direction you take, I recommend keeping the palette and shapes simple and subtle, and being sure your selection is in keeping with the style and scale of your home. As with many things in design, "less is more" applies.

AQUATIC PLANTS

A water garden indoors is truly unique and surprising. Placed in a transparent container, the forms of aquatic plants are suspended beneath the surface of the water while light filters gently through the container to cast shadows on the surrounding surfaces. Aquatic plants can be found at aquarium shops: a good shop will be able to direct you to the best kinds of plants for the application you choose. There are a few general categories (including those which float on the water's surface and those with roots below), but the plants I've used in these projects are known as true aquatics: they live completely submerged underwater. As far as particular varieties, I am partial to the round, disc-like leaves of pennywort, the way baby tears lie low around the bottom rocks, and the way the sculptural leaves of broad leaf swirl upward like green flames. Simple, tall glass vessels are the best containers because they provide a full view of the plant. Some enthusiasts employ air pumps and substrates in tanks for aquatic plants, but I've had long-lasting success without them following the basic care tips below. Typically the plants are sold with a little basket encasing their roots. This basket anchors easily under a layer of river stones to hold the plant in place in the container, although you may need a mix of both smaller and larger stones for the best results. All-black stones are appealing because they call to mind soil and contrast with the green of the plants well. Be mindful that once the container is filled with plants, stones, and water it will be heavy and difficult to move, so assemble it in its permanent location.

basic care Unlike an aquarium with a bubbling air pump, a glass container of aquatic plants has no aeration, so you'll need to completely replace the water over the course of a week. I do this by replacing one-quarter of the water daily with fresh water, not chlorinated or distilled water. To remove chlorine from your water, run it through a household filter like a Brita or leave a container of water standing overnight to evaporate the chlorine. I also recommend adding some aquatic plant fertilizer and liquid carbon (available at aquarium stores), as directed on the product packages. For most brands, a few drops every other day is all you will need. To limit algae growth, avoid placing aquatic gardens in direct sunlight; filtered sunlight is best.

DRIED & PRESSED MATERIALS

In one of the first plant-themed photoshoots I worked on, everything was dead and arranged with bones in a tableau similar to the 16th- and 17th-century *vanitas* style of European art meant to symbolize the fleetingness of life. While your own projects created with dried and pressed materials need not carry such intellectual weight, they are indeed a reminder of the transience of nature. The graphic forms of plants and flowers become more apparent when dried or pressed, and the colors mute to lovely hints of the original shades. With time and matter frozen, the plants can be studied and admired for years to come. While dried flowers may have a dusty or fussy association, there are many ways to style them that feel current and new. A great mass of baby's breath— yes, that clichéd florist's filler—looks shockingly contemporary as a cloud over a light fixture, while a garland crafted of dried pods and flower heads can be a talisman that feels both ancient and modern. Pressed flowers and fronds for projects are easy enough to make yourself in a flower press or between the pages of a telephone book (see page 138), or you can simply order them pre-pressed from a variety of sources. I especially like columbines for their fairy-like presence, the wispy fronds of tree ferns, the ghostly white color of dusty miller, and the graphic, cosmic starbursts of miniature Queen Anne's lace.

basic care Part of the appeal of dried and pressed materials is that they are low-maintenance. The type of project will determine any necessary care, but it should go without saying that dried and pressed botanicals should be kept in a dry place. Dried flowers and leaves that have maintained their original colors should be kept out of direct sunlight to avoid fading.

FERNS

In existence for nearly 300 million years, ferns do have an ancient air about them. Though seemingly simple in form, their leafy fronds are complex and geometric. Because most ferns can grow in low-light environments and like humidity, they are the model plant to use indoors. They look natural paired alongside their forest brethren, moss and lichens, and they are also striking in hanging pots. I find maidenhair ferns, with their finely cut leaves, especially beautiful. I also admire the wispy, feathery fronds of what is commonly known as asparagus fern (which isn't truly a fern, but looks as if it belongs in the category).

basic care Despite the wildness of their woodland home, ferns require some special attention to keep them looking their best indoors. Perhaps most important is moisture; while exact watering needs vary from fern to fern (and you should check the growing instructions for any variety you are considering planting), most require humidity in the air and consistently damp (but not wet) soil. If natural humidity is scarce in your home, misting periodically with room-temperature water will help. The second vital element for ferns is light—although they thrive in low-light environments, they do require sufficient light for photosynthesis. Place them near, but not in, a window—the trick is not to give them too much intense direct light, which can dry them out or burn their leaves.

MOSS & LICHENS

Moss and lichens are believed to pre-date even ferns by millions of years, so in working with them, you are working with some of the oldest types of living things on earth. The lush greens of different mosses and the spectrum of grays and greens of lichens are examples of nature's incredible palette. Though they are compatible aesthetically and can sometimes be found in similar locales, moss and lichen are not of the same family. Moss comes from spores while lichens are a composite organism that is part fungus and part bacteria or algae. To add to the confusion, the organism referred to as reindeer moss is actually a lichen, while Spanish moss is something else entirely, a bromeliad. But no matter—all make interesting materials for creating miniature landscapes in glass containers. Mosses are also useful as soil-toppers around potted plants to conceal the dirt, create natural-looking plantings, and help retain moisture. I especially like to pair a potted fern with pillow moss. Lichens are striking arranged on their own inside a glass jar, or mixed into a landscape with ferns and mosses. A note about acquiring moss and lichens: While it may seem harmless to forage mosses and lichens from their natural environments, the slow-growing organisms take a long time to regenerate and some areas have been over-harvested. Instead, it is more responsible to purchase cultivated varieties from reputable sources (see page 170). Like other plants, moss and lichens should never be removed from parks, national forests, or nature preserves.

basic care Mosses and lichens are available both live and dried. Some are sold dyed, but I recommend seeking out the undyed, natural versions. Specific projects might require variations in care, but, in general, live mosses need to be kept moist and well misted. As far as light is concerned, some mosses prefer sun and some prefer shade, so check with your source about what is best for your specimen. Dried lichens can be moistened a bit to restore their freshness and pliability.

SUCCULENTS & CACTI

Bold and geometric, succulents and cacti are the Brancusi sculptures of the natural world. There is a stoic stillness to their presence that I find calming in an interior and, because they are not leafy, they are a good choice for people who do not like regular houseplants. Beyond the common varieties, they are available in a multitude of shapes and sizes from specialty growers. The color palette of succulents is widely varied; I gravitate toward the ethereal gray, green, and purple tones. A single large plant can be incredible on its own, but I also like to see the various forms in a single planter with a mix of smaller varieties clustered together in families to create a kaleidoscopic effect. *Echeveria*, *Euphorbia*, and *Lithops* are some of my personal favorites. I prefer planting succulents and cacti in low-rimmed containers so they can rise above the edges to be fully admired.

basic care Once planted, succulents and cacti are very low maintenance. By design they are drought-tolerant, so if you are the type that often forgets to water, they are a good choice for you. They do require a considerable amount of light, so placement in a window with southern exposure (particularly in the winter) is preferable.

TILLANDSIA

Tillandsia plants are intriguing and sculptural in form. Their spiky leaves, sometimes thin and feathery, sometimes thicker and fleshy, stretch out in all directions in a wild, otherworldly fashion. There are dozens of varieties and many have a perfectly neutral, muted, matte gray-green color that suits many interiors. You can also find varieties that have hints of pale yellow, pink, or silvery purple. *Tillandsias* are commonly known as air plants because they appear to grow in thin air. They do not require soil and will survive in a variety of locations and situations, even set on a shelf or table or displayed in a glass container, as long as there is adequate circulation and regular watering. That they don't really require much in terms of care makes them ideal for the inexperienced indoor gardener or those without a lot of extra time. They are hardy, long lasting, and inexpensive. *Tillandsias* grow "pups," or shoots, which can be separated from the original plant and grown individually. Interestingly, the plants only bloom once in their lifetime, so if you happen to witness this moment, consider yourself lucky!

basic care In general most *Tillandsia* plants need bright, indirect sunlight found near a window. Soak them in water for about half an hour twice a week to keep them hydrated. Plan on morning baths: *Tillandsias* absorb the carbon monoxide from the air at night, and they cannot do so if the leaves are wet and cannot breathe. Shake away excess water and allow them to dry completely. Misting a few times a week between soaks will ensure that these plants don't dry out. Keep them away from air conditioners and heating devices, which can deplete moisture.

VINES

The thought of vines indoors might conjure an image of a mad tangle taking over a room, but they are a botanical decorating idea worth discovering. There are many ways to include vines in an interior. Traditional potted topiary can be relaxed into shapes beyond the classic ball by training them on a trellis of backyard twigs to control the chaos. And don't overlook cuttings of vines—you can use them to create arrangements in the same way you might utilize cut flowers. Even clippings of commonplace ivy can be arranged this way. A series of small vessels with vine cuttings spiraling out of them creates an un-fussy, minimalist elegance, and the trailing ends look lovely cascading over the edge of a shelf or mantel. When choosing vines, I am inclined to pick those with variegated leaves, but I also like the angel vine, which despite its tiny leaves is an extremely durable plant.

basic care Live potted vines should be maintained per the grower's instructions. Most flourish in bright light, and fast growers will need to be trimmed regularly to stay in shape. Watering needs of potted vines will vary by plant, but it's best to have a long-necked watering can with a narrow spout to be able to aim the water through the vines and into the pot to keep the leaves dry. For cut vines, change the water every day.

CONTAINERS
Botanicals and their containers have a symbiotic relationship: You should select the best combination of the two. I am drawn toward humble, straightforward materials such as simple clay, glass, and stone. I prefer basic shapes and finishes that walk the line

between modern and traditional. The tactile and emotional qualities of everyday objects also appeal to me; a glass jar or old compote can take on a new life for a special plant. Size and shape also play a role in selecting appropriate containers. Certain plants command specifics—aquatic plants need a cylindrical container with some height, for example, while others like *Tillandsia*, which can grow most anywhere, are more adaptable. Proportion might come into play: Low containers will make taller plants feel monumental, while taller vessels sometimes dwarf the plant. This is not necessarily a bad thing; try out different combinations to find the look you're after. You might discover that an unexpected shift in scale works the best.

READY—MADE CONTAINERS

A container does not need to be expensive to be practical and handsome. For ready-made clay pots and planters, I prefer black and gray clays or weathered terra cotta (as opposed to the more commonplace rusty orange) because they better complement the plants' forms and colors. A soft, matte white also looks graceful. Basic pots of stone or concrete are also good neutral bases. Glass is always a good choice for terrariums and water gardens.

HANDCRAFTED CONTAINERS

Constructing your own containers (or enhancing existing ones) brings a personal touch to a project. You can find supplies from your local hardware store to use in imaginative ways. You might commission a special container from an artisan to display a treasured plant, or creatively customize pots you already own.

FOUND CONTAINERS

Look around your home for vases, vessels, and bowls—all of these can serve as worthy vessels for your botanical creations. Even everyday glass bottles or jars can be repurposed and arranged artfully together. Remember, though, that multiples work best when the containers have some sort of relationship to one another, like a consistent material, color, or texture.

ESSENTIALS Here are the materials that (almost) every live plant needs. I've outlined the details in the individual projects, but this is a general guide to help you get started.

ACTIVATED HORTICULTURAL CARBON (CHARCOAL)

Available in either solid pieces or liquid form. While there are different theories on what carbon charcoal can or cannot do for your plants, I add a thin layer of the solid pieces in between the drainage stones and the soil to help maintain oxygen levels. Use the liquid form as directed on the package of the particular brand you purchase.

DRAINAGE STONES

Even when a pot has a drainage hole, I place a thin layer of stones in the bottom of a pot underneath the soil to allow water to drain through. Any kind of stones will do, even broken shards of terra cotta or pottery.

FERTILIZER

Most plants will benefit from a general plant fertilizer. Some types of plants require specialized fertilizer: cacti, *Tillandsia,* and aquatic plants are some examples. Be sure to consult the grower's instructions for your particular plant type.

SOIL

I always buy organic potting mixes. It's good to have a basic mix on hand for most potted projects, but some plants, like succulents, will require a specific potting mix specially formulated for their needs.

WATER

When watering, it's best to use room-temperature water so as not to shock the plants. Most tap water these days is chlorinated; leave some water standing overnight to de-chlorinate it (this is particularly important for water used with aquatic plants). Alternatively, you might use collected rainwater or filtered water.

SUPPORT MATERIALS These additional supplies provide important support for your plantings to keep the plants in place and stems upright. I avoid fancy accents—the idea is not to accessorize, but to keep the focus on the plants and their containers. I like to use natural materials whenever possible.

NATURAL TWIGS

Scavenged from your own backyard, a twig is an unobtrusive support when you need to help a stem stand straight. They can also be used to construct a mini trellis upon which a potted vine can climb.

RIVER STONES

These are used in water gardens to anchor aquatic plants in place inside glass vessels. Layered at the bottom of clear containers for drainage for potted plants or terrariums, I like the way the black stones blend seamlessly with soil to create a visually cohesive color base.

SAND

I use sand to create an aesthetically pleasing finishing top layer on the potting mixture for plantings of succulents or cacti. I prefer gray, natural, and black colors, available at your hardware store.

WAXED TWINE

In lieu of chunkier, more obtrusive hemp or sisal garden twine, waxed twine in gray, black, or green blends in when tying branches and stems in place for topiaries, or when tying stems to supports.

TOOL KIT It's not necessary to run out and purchase an entirely new set of tools for the projects in this book. Many of the tools are likely already in your home. While each project requires some specific supplies, here are a few essentials you'll need before you get started.

BAMBOO SKEWERS

Right out of the kitchen drawer, these multi-purpose sticks can be used to push leaves and stems out of the way when working in tight spaces with multiple plants or when trying to fit another plant into a pot or container. They can also be used as plant supports.

BAMBOO TONGS

Another kitchen item, these long tongs are easy to hold and the bamboo has a soft grip on plants. Use the tongs to adjust things inside a container when you cannot reach in with your hands.

BONSAI SHEARS

If you don't already own a pair, you may want to invest in good-quality Japanese shears. Sturdy and beautifully made, they are comfortable to hold and easily make clean cuts through live or dried stems and branches. They come in handy when arranging flowers or pruning, and their scaled-down size allows you to get into tight spots.

FORK

A regular table fork helps aerate the soil, and can be used to rake over the surface for a smooth finish once you have arranged everything.

GARDEN GLOVES

Although I prefer to work without them when handling soil, good gloves protect the hands when collecting gnarly branches and other specimens outside and when repotting cacti.

GARDEN SHEARS

An essential tool for clipping through stems and branches and pruning. Either have a pair of these on hand or, similarly, the bonsai shears described on the opposite page.

PLASTIC STRAW

I use straws to gently blow away dirt and sand from leaves and branches while creating landscapes.

SMALL PAINTBRUSH

A small, soft brush comes in handy for brushing away loose dirt and debris from the inside of container walls and from plants' foliage.

SPOON

Collect a few different sizes of spoons—larger spoons are good for scooping soil, while smaller spoons can aid in distributing soil into hard-to-reach places.

SPRAY BOTTLE OR MISTER

Essential for creating humidity for ferns, mosses, and air plants.

MAINTENANCE Once you have assessed, selected, assembled, and displayed a project, there is of course the aftercare required to keep it looking its best. The live botanical projects here are designed with minimal care in mind (a few, like the water gardens, are slightly more involved). They are living and growing, of course, so you will need to keep an eye on them. Different types of plants have different needs, but, in general, monitor the moisture levels of soil regularly, remove any decaying plants and leaves, and prune as necessary. You might find that a plant has outgrown its pot or container; you can always repot it in a larger vessel to use elsewhere and replace it with a smaller version in your original composition. When working with cut flowers in these projects, always give each stem a fresh cut on an angle—to expose a larger area for water intake—then immerse immediately in room temperature water. Be sure to remove any leaves from the stem that will be below the water line of your container to prevent rotting. To prolong the life of cut flowers, change the water daily and feed using 1 teaspoon of sugar per 1 cup/240 ml of water or a small amount of natural fertilizer; give each stem a fresh trim before re-inserting in the container.

PROJECTS

KNOTTED
ROPE PLANTER

There is something beautiful about the spatial lightness that a hanging plant creates in a room. With this project, I wanted to design a pared-down hanging planter, with one simple line of rope rather than the standard hanging pot set-up with several contact points around the edge of the pot. The ferns look less contained this way and can grow freely. Here, essential materials—rope, clay, and a maidenhair fern—combine for a minimalist display.

—

TIP The rope is threaded through a length of PVC piping within the pot to protect it from disintegrating in the soil. Choose a width of rope that will be able to comfortably pass through the drainage hole of your pot, and plants that are bushy enough to conceal a part of the rope.

TIP Hanging the planter from your ceiling can be tricky; it's best to have someone else to help.

materials

Ceiling hook and anchor

Wall hook (optional)

Ruler or tape measure

Several lengths of ¾-in-/2-cm-thick
Manila rope

Pocketknife

15-in-/38-cm-long agg tooth saw
or hacksaw

1½-in-/3.5-cm-wide PVC piping

Weathered terra-cotta pot, 10 in/
25 cm high with an 8-in-/20-cm-
round opening

Drainage stones

Activated horticultural carbon

Soil scoop or spoon

Potting soil

Two maidenhair ferns

Scissors

5-ply natural jute twine

continued

ASSEMBLY

1 Install the ceiling hook and anchor, and the wall hook if desired. Measure the distance from desired bottom of pot to ceiling height (remember you'll want to be able to easily water the plant), add the distance from ceiling hook to wall hook including drape (ours adds 1 ft/30 cm of slack), and distance from wall hook to floor. Add approximately 30 in/75 cm to allow for the knot below the pot and the coiled rope on the floor. Cut rope to approximate size with the pocketknife (you can always trim off some from the end later if need be).

2 Cut a length of PVC pipe 2 in/5 cm shorter than your pot with an agg tooth saw.

3 Holding the pipe in place above the drainage hole, begin to prepare the pot for planting. Place about 1 in/2.5 cm of stones at the bottom of the pot for drainage and sprinkle a light layer of horticultural carbon over the stones to keep the soil fresh.

4 Spoon potting soil into the pot, then place the two ferns around the center pipe. Continue to fill the pot with soil securely around the plants and pipe.

5 Thread one end of the rope through the exposed top of the piping, then out through the drainage hole in the bottom. Tie a knot in the rope so that it rests against the bottom of the pot, with a 4-in/10-cm tail.

6 Cut 1 yd/1 m of twine with the scissors and use it to tie a whipping knot around the tail of the rope knot for a clean finish and to prevent it from unraveling. You can find directions for tying whipping knots online.

7 With a helper holding the pot, position the rope onto the hook in the desired spot and tie a knot to secure it in place. Drape the rest of the rope across to the wall hook, and let the end fall into a puddle on the floor. I like this longer length, but you could just as well cut a shorter length that just hangs down from the ceiling.

—

care

There is no need to remove the pot from the hook for watering. Maidenhair ferns prefer consistently moist soil, so water often with small amounts of water. If you use another type of plant, you may wish to place a bucket underneath the pot when watering.

GILDED
BONSAI VITRINE

Much like a glass vitrine cabinet holding jewels or objets d'art, this gilded temple-like structure serves as the perfect jewel-box surrounding a peaceful moment. Creating architecture around a bonsai is similar to framing artwork: it elevates the plant into a whole other object entirely. The gold leafing on this project adds a subtle bit of luxury. This is a very special creation—it would make an impressive centerpiece on a large table or serve as a soothing vision to wake to every day on a nightstand in a bedroom.

—

TIP This clear acrylic vitrine was made to measure in a 6-by-6-by-12-in/15-cm-by-15-cm-by-30-cm size (find my source on page 171); you could have a similar box made by a local glazier in whatever size you like. Ready-made large-size clear vessels aren't so easy to find, but if you can't go custom, a good alternative might be a small vintage fish tank. Be sure your vitrine is made with enough room to accommodate future growth (at the very least, allow a little more than half the height of the bonsai). The bonsai does not have to fit perfectly inside; in fact, it's more interesting if it creeps out a little at the front. I selected a bonsai, but of course a vitrine can be used to display any type of plant.

materials

Small paintbrush

Gold leaf kit

Clear rectangular acrylic vitrine

4- to 5-in-/10- to 13-cm-tall bonsai

Small ceramic or porcelain bowl

Bonsai potting soil

continued

ASSEMBLY

1 Work on applying gold leaf to one edge of the vitrine at a time. Using a small paintbrush, lightly brush gold leaf sizing along one edge of the vitrine opening around the inside and outside edges. The sizing line need not be perfect, but aim for about ¼ to ½ in/0.5 cm to 1.5 cm on the inside and outside edges.

2 Holding a book of gold leaf in your hand, carefully fold back the protective paper to expose the leaf. Lay the leaf on the sized area on the rim and let it attach to the sizing on the inside and outside. Smooth the leaf down with the paintbrush and let it set, then pull the leaf away slightly to make pretty, irregular edges. The goal is to have it look somewhat rough-hewn.

3 Continue applying leaf around the entire opening of the vitrine. Take pieces that break off and gingerly use them to fill in spots that you may miss.

4 Allow the leaf to dry completely (about 30 to 40 minutes), then brush away the loose bits of gold leaf with the small paintbrush. Reapply sizing and leaf to any spots you may have missed.

5 Repot the bonsai according to the grower's instructions into a container of approximately the same size as its original vessel, adding more soil as needed. Place inside your vitrine.

—

care

For the vitrine: Glass cleaner and paper towels can mar the acrylic. If you need to clean the panels, try a mixture of white vinegar and water applied with a soft, clean cloth.

For the bonsai: The ideal indoor placement is near a windowsill facing south; an east or west exposure is second best. A minimum of four to six hours of sunlight per day is recommended. Water when the soil appears dry, but never allow the soil to become completely dried out. I suggest fertilizing at half the suggested strength using a general liquid fertilizer. Most bonsai trees have already been through their training period, thus requiring only periodic trimming or pinching of the limbs to maintain their form.

N.^o **3**

FLOWERING BRANCH
WALL SCONCE

I've often admired vintage floral metalwork wall sconces I've seen at flea markets and antiques stores. Here, I've translated the concept using natural materials for an earthier, more ethereal feeling. In reality, this branch is a fantasy, as strawflowers do not grow on branches, but it does bring life to a space with its unusual matte, monochromatic effect. And, unlike spring's fleeting flowering branches of quince and cherry, this one can be enjoyed all year, anywhere in your home.

—

TIP Fallen backyard branches make a good base for the sconce. Look for a branch with a nice spreading shape to it; you may need to clip a few bits so the branch lies flat against the wall.

TIP I used dried heads of *Helichrysum* flowers (commonly known as strawflowers or everlastings), but you can use whatever variety of dried flower you like. If you are buying yours pre-dried, get more than you think you will need, as you may have to edit out a few less-desirable blooms from the bunches. The number you will need depends on the size of the branch you have and how full you'd like it to look.

materials

Found branch

Garden shears

Tarp or newspapers

Matte spray paint in a bone white color

Dried flowers

Tacky craft glue

Gray waxed twine

Hammer and small nail

continued

ASSEMBLY

1 Find a backyard branch. Look for a shape you can imagine hanging on your wall; a central vertical line and two lines branching off is ideal, but you can trim what you find to size.

2 Working outside, lay down the tarp or newspaper. Place the branch on top and spray paint it according to the manufacturer's instructions until it is completely covered. Let dry for about 30 minutes.

3 Snip the flower heads from the stems.

4 Lay the branch flat on your workspace. Apply a dot of glue for each flower head to spots on the ends of the twigs where blooms would naturally appear and in a few places along the branches till you have a nice, full "blooming" look.

5 Tie a loop of waxed twine for hanging where it can rest under a branching point, about 6 to 8 in/15 to 20 cm up from the bottom of the stem. The waxed twine has a grip to it that will help hold it in place on the branch once the loop is placed over a nail. Hammer the nail into the wall and install.

—

care

Should the sconce get a bit dusty, just give it a little dusting with a small soft paintbrush. If a flower or branch breaks off, simply glue it back into place.

TILLANDSIA GARLAND

Part sculpture and part living, growing thing, a garland of *Tillandsia* is unexpected and intriguing in your home. The vertical positioning and clear hanging filament make it seem suspended in midair. There really is no other plant that could do this. There are so many varieties available; I have several favorites—and this is a good way to display nearly all of them. Look for the *T. stricta* *'Purple,'* *T. ionatha* *'Zebrina,'* *T. concolor* *'Strepto,'* and *T. vernicosa* varieties.

—

TIP Monofilament fishing line is so thin it's practically invisible, but it's strong enough to hold the weight of the plants.

materials

Small ceiling hook

Scissors

5 yd/5 m of 6-lb-/2.7-kg-test clear
    monofilament fishing line

Assorted *Tillandsia* in varied shapes
    and sizes (approximately 12 plants
    for a 9-ft-/3-m-high ceiling)

continued

ASSEMBLY

1 Choose a place to hang the garland where it can be enjoyed but won't get in the way, like the corner of a room or tucked into a stairwell. Install the hook into position on your ceiling, then determine how long you'd like your garland to be.

2 Cut about 15 ft/4.5 m of the monofilament line to work with (you can always trim off the remainder at the end).

3 Working on the floor, lay out your selection of *Tillandsia* plants to make sure you like the arrangement. Try to space out larger specimens so they don't seem clumped in one spot. Consider how you'd like to position each plant on the line—vertically or horizontally—and space them roughly 5 to 7 in/13 to 18 cm apart depending on the size of the plant. Allow enough space in between the plants so that they don't touch.

4 Starting with the bottom plant, begin to tie the *Tillandsias* to the line. Simply wrap a bit of the line around the plant in between its leaves and tie a single or double knot to secure it in place.

5 When you finish stringing the plants, check the line length, then make a hanging loop, knot it, and cut any excess line. Be sure to make your loop large enough to remove the garland for watering.

—

care

Hang the garland in bright, indirect light. Twice a week, take it off the hook and lower it gently into a bucket of room-temperature filtered water for about half an hour. Be mindful not to tangle the line. Shake each plant a bit to remove any water between the leaves and let the garland dry on a towel before re-installing. Mist with water a few times in between waterings. Fertilize as directed for your varieties.

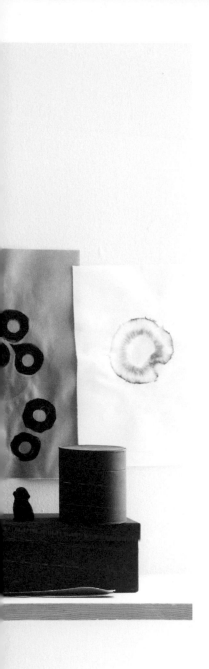

Nº **5**

MUSHROOM SPORE PRINTS

At first glance, the origin of these mysterious inky blots may be unclear. They're printed using the undersides of mushroom caps— the spores leave their mark on the paper in wonderfully fluid organic shapes resembling watercolors. Depending on the density of the spores, some of the prints will be defined, while others will be very dark. If you're lucky, the lines of the individual gills, or *lamellae*, will be visible. I like their abstract shapes and sepia tones, and prefer to display them in an ensemble, casually left unframed.

—

TIP For best results, choose specimens with intact gills—I find that mushrooms sourced at a farmers' market are the freshest and least damaged. You can also experiment with mushrooms you find in the wild, but be aware that some species have white spores, which might not show up on lighter-colored paper. The mushrooms should be mature, with no edges ("veils") covering their gills underneath or the spores won't fully release. I used smaller and larger examples of the species *Agaricus bisporus*, which includes common button mushrooms, creminis, and portobellos. Your specimens need not be perfectly round in shape; in fact, a few irregularities make for a more interesting print.

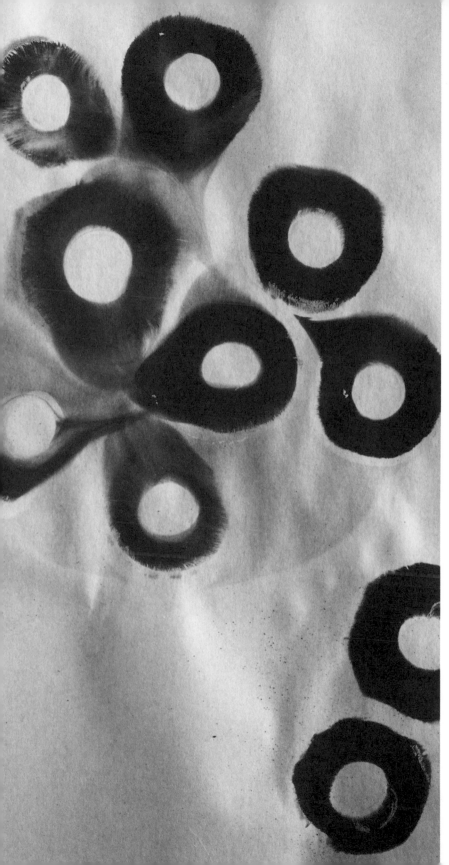

materials

Knife

Fresh, mature mushrooms

Sheets of heavy, acid-free artist paper
 in white, gray, or lavender

Bowls or cups large enough to cover
 mushrooms singularly or in groups

continued

1 Use the knife to remove the stem of the mushroom as near to its base as possible. Be careful not to damage the gills in the process.

2 Place the cap, gills-side down, onto the paper. You may wish to print the image of one mushroom or several at a time.

3 Cover the mushroom cap with a bowl completely so it won't be disturbed and to protect it from breezes. Some mushrooms might produce prints in a few hours, but it's best to leave the mushroom undisturbed overnight for best results.

4 Remove the bowl, then, with a gentle, steady motion, remove the mushroom cap. Allow the paper to dry flat completely for a few hours before hanging.

—

care

Spore prints are delicate. I recommend applying a drawing fixative—an easy-to-use spray (available at art supply stores) that artists apply to pencil and charcoal drawings to prevent smudging. A few imperfections are okay; they will all have natural inconsistencies, but it's best to fix them if you would like to keep the prints for a while. Follow the directions, and simply lay the prints out on a protected surface (outside, if possible, for ventilation) and lightly apply two coats. Allow to dry for the time specified on the fixative package between coats. Should you decide to store the prints, place a piece of smooth glassine in between each print to prevent rubbing and smudging. The prints should last indefinitely, especially if you have used acid-free art paper. If you haven't, the paper might yellow slightly, but that will give your prints a vintage beauty.

№ **6**

BABY'S TEARS
CENTERPIECE

Named for the appearance of its tiny leaves, baby's tears (*Helxine soleirolii*) is a compact creeping herb of Mediterranean origin that has long been valued for its ornamental appeal. Grouped en masse along the center of a table, the plant's luxurious texture and vivid color resemble a verdant field of little green hills.

—

TIP This lush plant puts a collection of simple yet pretty ceramic and porcelain tableware to good use. Because they are low growers, baby's tears won't obstruct the view of your dining companions across the table, making it the perfect centerpiece.

materials

Assorted low dishes, compotes, bowls

Drainage stones (about ¾ cup/175 ml
  per small container)

Activated horticultural carbon (about
  1 tbsp/15 ml per container)

Potting soil

Baby's tears plants

continued

ASSEMBLY

1 Arrange a grouping of containers you like. For this type of plant, I like to mix higher compotes with lower bowls, all in complementary, but not matching, colors. There should be a comfortable flow to the lineup.

2 Prepare the containers for planting. First, insert a layer of drainage stones, then a thin layer of horticultural carbon. Add a small amount of soil, leaving enough room to accommodate the roots of the baby's tears.

3 Add the plant, and fill in with soil around the sides.

—

care

Baby's tears is very tolerant of filtered, indirect light, which makes it an ideal indoor plant. The plants like moisture; care for them as you would any dish garden or terrarium, keeping the soil moist but not soggy. Check the moisture level with your fingertip every other day, and be careful not to overwater, as there are no drainage holes. As the plants grow, they will slowly creep over the edges of the containers and might need a trim. Once they have completely overgrown the vessels, you can separate them at the roots and replant in other pots following the instructions above.

7

MOUNTED FUNGI
SPECIMEN DISPLAY

Known as conks, these bracket fungi and horse's hoof fungi specimens have strangely beautiful colors and textures. On the upper side, you can sometimes see concentric striations representing years of growth like tree rings. I chose a selection of horse's hoof and varnished shelf fungi for this project. I love them simply mounted on an unfinished board, as a contemporary version of what you might find in a natural history museum.

—

TIP Often found growing on dead trees in the forest, woody bracket fungi are also available dried and ready for crafting—you'll find my favorite source on page 170.

TIP Wooden art boards are sold online and in art-supply shops in many precut sizes; I used a fairly large piece here, but you can choose whatever size you like.

materials

Dried bracket fungi

Rough sandpaper

17¾-by-23¾-in/45-cm-by-60-cm wood
   art board

Hot glue gun

continued

ASSEMBLY

1 Prepare the fungi for mounting by lightly sanding the back with rough sandpaper to flatten them.

2 Lay the board flat on your workspace, and experiment with positioning to figure out the layout for your display before you start to glue.

3 Apply hot glue in a zigzag pattern on the back of each fungus and press it onto the board. Allow to dry.

—

care

The board can either be casually propped against a wall or hung with a hook. A careful dry dusting with a feather duster every once in a while should be enough to keep them looking their best.

8

SUCCULENT
STONE GARDEN

There is something about succulents that feels from another era. They have a prehistoric quality, so it seems only fitting to plant them in a monolithic-style stone planter, as if they have sprung up among ancient ruins. Here, inexpensive concrete paving slabs from a home renovation store are transformed into a handsome planter holding a mix of sedums, lithops, and echeveria. I like to create two of these planters to display together as a striking pair.

—

TIP   To fill these with an abundance of as many different varieties of succulents as possible, try to find the smallest you can get to fit the most in (you may want to call the supplier to ensure you get the smallest available at a particular time of year). It is fine to plant them close together as they grow quite slowly and will take some time to fill in.

materials

FOR EACH PLANTER:

Three 5½-in./14-cm-square paving
  stones (to make two sides and
  the bottom)

Two 5½-by-8-in/14-cm-by-20-cm
  rectangular paving stones (to make
  the two longer sides)

Liquid Nails

2-in./5-cm-wide duct tape

Plastic carrier bag to use as a liner

Scissors

Small drainage stones

Cactus/succulent potting soil

Assorted small sedums, lithops, and
  echeveria (approximately 25 plants)

Small spoon or chopstick

Soft paintbrush

continued

1 Assemble the planter. Lay the paving stones backside up as shown. Apply Liquid Nails adhesive to each paving stone as shown, approximately ¾ in/2 cm in from the edge.

2 Starting with the square stones, press the stones into place verti-cally one at a time (they will stand upright on their own). Then wrap entire planter in duct tape as shown to hold the stones in place while the adhesive dries overnight.

3 Once the planter is complete and the adhesive has dried, remove the duct tape. Fit the plastic carrier bag in the bottom and cut it so it sits about 1 in/2.5 cm below the top of the planter.

4 Fill the liner bag with about 1½ in/4 cm of drainage stones at the bottom, then the potting soil.

5 Sort out the arrangement of the plants while they are still in their original containers, being mindful of both color and form. You want to be able to see the shapes of all the plants even though they are close together; avoid placing all of the taller plants in one spot, and instead work toward an even distribution of sizes.

continued

6 Begin planting in the center and work your way out toward the edges. To unpot the succulents, gently squeeze around their containers until the root ball loosens and the plant can be removed. Use a small spoon or a bamboo skewer to make little holes for the plants to rest in, and then move the soil back around the base of the plant.

7 Once you have planted everything, gently brush off any soil caught in the plants with the paintbrush.

—

care

Water as needed. Place in a sunny location near a window with southern exposure. Routinely check the moisture level of the soil using your fingertip and water carefully as this style of "dish garden" has no drain holes.

N<u>o</u> **9**

GYPSOPHILA SPHERE

This ethereal globe–like sculpture has a celestial presence; it's light as air, but explosive at the same time. I have always loved the fine and light texture of *Gypsophila*, more commonly known as baby's breath. While it tends to be overused as filler in standard–issue flower arrangements, it is underused as a decorative element in its own right. And since it's inexpensive, you can use great masses of it. The completed sphere is magical as is, but it will glow from within beautifully should you choose to light it.

—

TIP   This sphere was created using eight bunches of baby's breath and a very large (20 in/50 cm) paper lantern, but the technique can be used to make one of any size. A large lantern might need a few days to complete, while a smaller size can be made in a few hours.

TIP   You can buy pre-dried baby's breath for ease or to save time, but buying it live and drying it yourself (hang bunches upside down to dry) is not difficult and might yield better results as it dries in a more natural form and is not damaged in shipping.

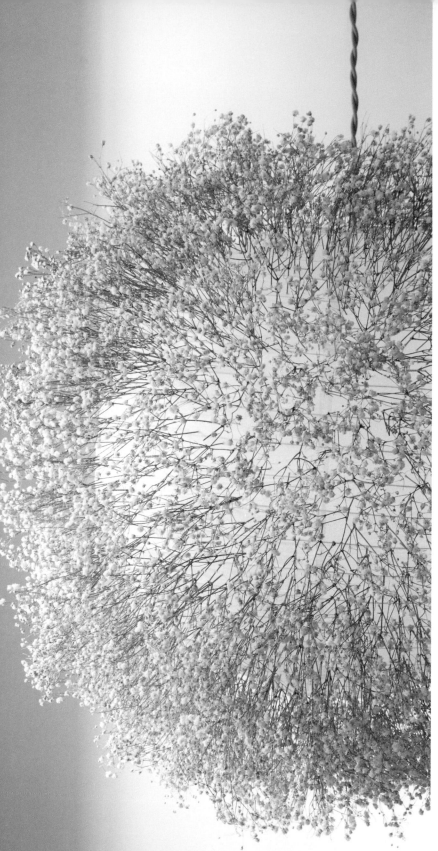

materials

Ceiling hook and anchor

Spherical paper lantern

Lamp cord, or string or cord
  for hanging

Dried baby's breath

Garden shears or wire cutter

Hot glue gun

continued

ASSEMBLY

1 Install the ceiling hook and anchor where you plan to display the sphere. If you plan on illuminating the sphere, put the lamp cord in place in the lantern before you begin. If not, you can simply cut a length of string or cord as desired and tie it to the top of the lantern for hanging. You will need to work with the lantern within reach—either hanging in its permanent position but lowered to a comfortable level, or hanging elsewhere, in which case you will need to carefully move it to its final location when complete. I recommend standing while you work, if possible, so you can easily move around the lantern.

2 Prepare the baby's breath stems by trimming them down to about 4 in/10 cm in length. Work with one bunch at a time to keep your work area tidy.

3 Starting at the top of the lantern around the perimeter of the opening, begin to attach the ends of the individual stems to the lantern. Touch the bottom of the stem to the hot glue gun nozzle to add a tiny amount of glue to the bottom, then hold the stem end perpendicular to the surface of the lantern for a few seconds while the glue dries.

4 Continue working around the circumference of the lantern toward the bottom, making sure the blooms are filling in nicely. The stems should be about 1 to 2 in/2.5 to 5 cm apart depending on the amount of blooms per stem. As you reach the bottom, you may need to work from beneath the lantern to finish.

—

care

The finished sphere is very fragile, so avoid moving it once it is complete. It requires no further care and should last indefinitely if left untouched.

FERN MOUND

A welcoming tableau at the foot of the stairs or an entryway, this feathery asparagus fern atop a mound of moss looks like a miniature scene from a Chinese landscape painting. The solid, modern-looking black terrazzo cube planter is a good foil for its delicate contents and contrasts with the greens to make them look especially verdant and lush.

—

TIP Live moss is available from many growers—see the Sources section on page 170 for some of my favorite suppliers. Pillow moss (also called cushion moss) is a light green color with a silvery-white cast and grows in a round cushion shape, while mood moss grows in a very compact clump with very feathery plumes sprouting out.

materials

12-in-/30-cm-square modern
  cube planter
Drainage stones
Activated horticultural carbon
Potting soil
Asparagus fern
Mood or pillow moss
Small soft paintbrush

continued

ASSEMBLY

1 Prepare the planter. First put in a layer of drainage stones, about 1 in/2.5 cm thick, then a thin layer of horticultural carbon.

2 Add soil, leaving enough room near the top of the vessel (about 2 to 3 in/5 to 7.5 cm, depending on the thickness of the moss) to add the asparagus fern and the mounds of moss.

3 Position the asparagus fern first. I prefer to plant this slightly off-center to create an asymmetrical arrangement. Lightly squeeze the original pot to loosen the soil so the plant comes out. Use your hands to gently loosen the root ball a bit and replant the fern into a hole in the soil in the new vessel. Cover root ball with soil up to the base of the stems.

4 Surround the fern with pieces of moss. Press the moss firmly into place in the soil. The edges where the pieces meet will form nice mounded shapes like rolling hills. Break off small pieces to fill in where you need to, and fill in the top completely.

5 Brush off any dirt or debris with a soft brush.

—

care

An asparagus fern and moss will do well in filtered light; too much sun will turn the fronds of the fern yellow and dry out the moss. Mist and gently sprinkle the moss with water; it does not appreciate being soaked. Water the fern directly near the base of the plant once or twice a week depending on the heat and humidity in your home.

cut vine tableau

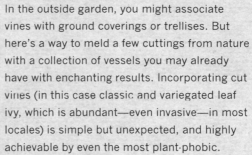

In the outside garden, you might associate vines with ground coverings or trellises. But here's a way to meld a few cuttings from nature with a collection of vessels you may already have with enchanting results. Incorporating cut vines (in this case classic and variegated leaf ivy, which is abundant—even invasive—in most locales) is simple but unexpected, and highly achievable by even the most plant-phobic.

A series of containers like these vintage glass laboratory beakers, bottles, and vases brings new meaning to the idea of a "floral arrangement" and breaks free of the static notion that one container can tell the whole story. Warm water, soap, and a bit of rubbing alcohol will remove any stubborn labels from repurposed containers. I liked the purity of this clear glass arrangement, but adding colored glass to the mixture could be beautiful as well.

Arrange your vessels at different heights and sizes. Fill them with water. Isolate a few lyrical vines and vary them so that some stand vertical while others trail. Not every container needs a cutting. You may need to trim away a few leaves in order for the cutting to fit into the vessel, but it is also nice to see a few leaves inside the wider containers if they fit. The arrangement should last a couple of weeks if you replace the water every other day.

No 11

CRYSTAL-ENCRUSTED PLANTER

This crystal-encrusted planter proves that common houseplants don't have to be dowdy; it *is* possible to dress them up in some finery. In creating this project I was inspired by the great garden grottoes of 16th-century Italy and France, which featured shells and faux geological compositions, and I wanted to bring their outdoor beauty inside. *Hypoestes phyllostachya*, or polka-dot plant, is widely available at garden centers and home improvement stores—I prefer the pink variety, which has radical patterning on its leaves, as a more unusual alternative to green foliage.

materials

10-in-square-by-2¾-in-high/25-cm-
   square-by-7-cm-high cement or
   ceramic planter

Sobo craft glue

3½-lb/1.5-kg jar of clear sea glass
   crystals (1⅛-in./3-cm-size pieces)
   for planter exterior

Towel

5 cups/1 L of gravel for drainage

Activated horticultural carbon

Peat moss–based potting soil

3 pink *Hypoestes phyllostachya*
   (polka-dot plants)

Spoon

ADDITIONAL OPTIONAL
GROUND COVER DECORATIONS:*

3½-lb/1.5-kg jar of clear sea glass
   crystals (1⅛-in./3-cm-size pieces)

3½ lb/1.5 kg jar of light pink sea glass
   crystals (1⅛-in./3-cm-size pieces)

1 or 2 larger decorative crystals

*Note: As listed, these are the smallest amounts
available for these items, but you will not use the
entire quantity. Save the extras for other projects.

continued

ASSEMBLY

1 Working on one side of the planter at a time, glue the clear glass crystals to the outer walls and allow each side to dry before moving on to the next. To begin, stand the planter on one of its sides (the sea glass will adhere better on a flat surface). Working from the base up to the top edge, begin gluing the clear glass crystals to the exterior, fitting irregular pieces into place as you go. Once the side is completely covered, fill in with smaller pieces and be sure to also place some pieces around the top edge of the planter. Allow it to dry about 3 hours.

2 Create a base to hold the planter upright for further gluing by scrunching up a towel. Place the planter securely on the towel, and continue the process of gluing and drying each side until all four are covered. You can place the towel and planter inside a bin or box to hold the planter upright while it is drying.

3 Once the planter is covered with crystals, prepare it for planting. Place a ¾-in/2-cm layer of gravel in the bottom, then a thin layer of the horticultural carbon. Add enough soil to be able to anchor the roots of the plants; you may raise the soil level slightly above the rim of the container to gain more root space.

4 Position the plants in the soil in an asymmetrical triangular arrangement, leaving enough room to see a little bit of soil in between them. Once the plants are in place, fill in with additional soil.

5 Create a decorative ground cover using the materials of your choice. Alternate patches of clear and pink sea glass until the entire surface of the soil is covered in a rich layer of texture. A spoon is helpful when placing glass pieces in awkward-to-reach spots between plants and foliage. Finish with a couple of standing crystals if desired.

care

Place your completed planter where it will get plenty of light, but out of direct sun. Filtered light from a south- or west-facing window is ideal. Leaves on the polka-dot plant may turn to solid green in low light. These tropical natives enjoy being grouped together as it helps maintain their humidity levels. To water, you'll need to gently move away a small area of the decorative groundcover near the stem bases, and add water with an eyedropper or small spoon; this will help preserve the decorative ground cover arrangement. Keep the soil lightly moist, taking care not to overwater. If the leaves begin to yellow, the soil is too soggy. To maintain the small bushy scale of the polka-dot plant, pinch off taller stems to encourage lower stems to branch out. Purple flowers may appear and should be pinched off because they will deplete the foliage and cause the plant to deteriorate after they have bloomed. Fertilize with a liquid fertilizer once a month.

The plants will eventually outgrow the planter; replace them with younger plants or you can root plants from stem cuttings of the originals.

№ **12**

TILLANDSIA
PEDESTALS

Traveling in a remote area of the Dominican Republic, I came upon an incredible sight— massive *Tillandsia* growing in the trees. These *Tillandsia* pedestals are an indoor translation of that tropical beauty. By their very design, *Tillandsia* are sculptural. With no need for soil they are quite happy to perch atop something, and a pedestal presentation will accentuate their eccentric foliage to full effect. The pedestal base doesn't need to be anything more than a beautiful piece of wood, and you can display the *Tillandsia* pedestals singularly or in a series unified by the plants' color palette. I especially like larger varieties such as the *Tillandsia xerographica* and *Tillandsia leonamiana* shown here.

—

TIP Floral suppliers and garden shops carry all manner of different wood pieces, or you can just trim down a found piece of wood.

materials

Larger varieties of *Tillandsia*

Wood bases

Saw (optional)

continued

1 Choose your *Tillandsia*. If you are displaying in groupings, consider looking for an assortment of leaf shapes connected by similar colors.

2 Select a wood base. Be resourceful with what you might have around the house or can find outside—a small piece of firewood, a fallen log, driftwood.

3 To prevent the base from moving, you may need to saw a flat edge on the bottom.

4 Pair the *Tillandsia* with an appropriate wood base. Choose your plant and look for a natural spot on the base to place it—a notch is a good place to nestle some plants, others can simply rest on top.

care

Display in bright, indirect sunlight near a window but away from heating and cooling devices. Twice a week, soak each plant in water for about half an hour to keep them hydrated; shake away excess water and allow to dry completely. Mist a few times a week in between soaks. Add bromeliad fertilizer to the watering as per manufacturer's instructions. With good care, the plants should last several years.

GEOMETRIC BOTANICAL SCULPTURE

For centuries, people have tried to tame the wildness of natural plant life in different ways, such as topiary and espaliers. Inspired by the bold sculptures of artists Tony Smith and Constantin Brancusi, I wanted to make a modern interpretation of this idea in a new kind of arrangement by using organic textures on top of geometric forms. I chose dried flowers for this project, but you could easily do it with fresh if you prefer. Either way, you are exploring nature sculpturally through color, scale, texture, and form. This sculpture might be made for a special occasion, or simply placed as a decorative object on a bookshelf, side table, credenza, or mantel.

materials

4-pack Oasis Sahara dry floral foam
   bricks (each brick measures 3 by
   4 by 9 in/7.5 by 10 by 23 cm)

Ruler

Serrated bread knife

FloraCraft StyroGlue

4-in-/10-cm-square by 4-in-/10-cm-
   square cement vase

Toothpicks

6 bunches of dried hill flowers (salmon,
   or color of choice)

2 bunches of dried hill flowers (beige)

Garden shears

continued

TIP Oasis foam is commonly used by florists to anchor flower stems in arrangements; here, I use it as a base for the sculpture as it is lightweight and easy to manipulate into different shapes. Some Oasis foams are moistened to keep flowers hydrated; the kind I used here, Sahara, is used dry. Oasis is sold in large blocks, but it is easy to cut to whatever size and shape you prefer using a serrated bread knife. For this sculpture I used three rectangle blocks measuring 3 by 4 by 2 in/7.5 by 10 by 5 cm, one rectangle block measuring 2½ by 3½ by 4½ in/6 by 9 by 11.5 cm, and one larger rectangle block measuring 6 by 4 by 6 in/15 by 10 by 15 cm (made of two 3-by-4-by-6-in/7.5-by-10-by-15-cm pieces glued together). The sizing and placement is only a suggestion—feel free to experiment with your own foam compositions. When cutting, do not saw back and forth; instead, slowly slice through the foam with a seesaw motion, being careful to cut straight down until the foam splits.

TIP Before assembling the sculpture with the StyroGlue (a water-based styrofoam adhesive), you may first want to set the placement of the floral foam with toothpicks, then secure with the StyroGlue once you're satisfied. Let the edges of the smaller forms extend beyond the base to create the illusion of an asymmetrical balancing form.

ASSEMBLY

1 Prepare the floral foam base. Using the ruler and serrated knife, measure and cut one 3-by-4-by-6-in/7.5-by-10-by-15-cm piece from one of the foam bricks, then cut a second piece of the same size from one of the other bricks. Reserve the leftovers. Use the StyroGlue to glue the two pieces together lengthwise to make a block that measures 6-by-4-by-6-in/15-by-10-by-15-cm. Let dry for 2 to 3 hours.

2 Prepare the secondary floral foam pieces. Using the ruler and serrated knife, measure and cut three 2½-by-3½-by-2-in/6-by-9-by-5-cm pieces and one 2½-by-3½-by-4½-in/6-by-9-by-11.5-cm piece from the remaining foam.

3 Assemble the sculpture. Center the floral foam base over the top of the vase with the 6-in./15-cm-long side facing you to check placement. Remove the foam base, and apply the StyroGlue around the top edge of the vase. Put the floral foam base back into place on top of the vase and allow glue to dry about 2 hours.

4 Working piece by piece, use the toothpicks to position the three smaller secondary floral foam pieces on the front, right, and back side of the base at varying levels to make an asymmetrical composition. Allow the edges of the secondary pieces to extend beyond the base. When you are pleased with the composition, secure each piece in place with StyroGlue.

5 Position the final piece on top of the base, again allowing it to extend beyond the edge, and glue into place. Allow to dry 2 to 3 hours.

6 Prepare the dried flowers for placement. Use the garden shears to trim the stems to 1 in/2.5 cm at a diagonal to better pierce the foam.

7 Working in sections, apply small amounts of StyroGlue to the sculpture and insert the stem ends of the flower heads into the foam to cover the surface as shown. Fill in the surface organically (not in rows) to avoid too rigid of a pattern; do not leave any gaps where the floral foam would show through. Let dry 2 to 3 hours.

—

care

With dried flowers, the sculpture should last indefinitely. A light brushing with a soft paintbrush will keep it dust free.

№ 14

WOODLAND WORLD

Here is a still life of lush color and texture from the outdoors, idealized and contained. Finding the bits of forest ephemera is an enjoyable part of the process—look closely at the ground to find the smaller details of nature that usually go unnoticed, like the moss and pebbles that collect around the roots of trees or fallen trunks. Though displayed in a covered glass jar, this magical assemblage is not a true planted terrarium, but more of an arrangement.

—

TIP To find the contents for this container, I explored the forest floor on a friend's land, but you could gather similar specimens from the wilds of your own backyard. Be sure to only take a small amount from your own property, and never from public parks or protected areas as mosses and lichens take a long time to recover.

materials

Covered glass container, suitably sized
  for your chosen items
Assorted woodland specimens—twigs,
  branches, lichen, moss, pinecones
  or pods

continued

ASSEMBLY

1 Clean the glass container, being sure to rinse it thoroughly, and allow it to dry.

2 Collect your specimens.

3 Fill the container. You can establish the arrangement with a larger piece like a moss-covered chunk of wood or stone, or a couple of large river stones you already have.

4 When you are happy with the base, add smaller found elements such as fallen twigs covered in lichen, small tufts of moss (do not disrupt large moss colonies), and pinecones or pods. Handle everything gently, and once the elements are inside the vessel it's best to leave it alone.

—

care

Place the jar in indirect light and keep watch to monitor the moisture levels for any live elements like moss or ferns that you include; if it's too dry, lightly mist with water, but if you see any mildew start to form, remove the infected pieces immediately and leave the cover off for several hours to allow the elements to breathe a bit. Other elements, like lichen on twigs, will simply dry and require no further care.

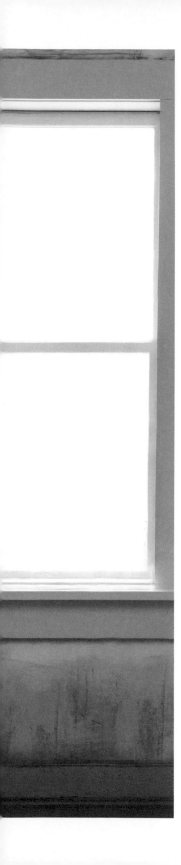

BRAIDED
WILLOW WREATH

A bunch of fresh willow cuttings inspired this project, which reinvents a traditional wreath from the perfectly formed circle of green to something wilder. It resembles a giant charcoal scribble on a wall with its wispy, sketchy lines. The unusually large scale of the finished oval has amazing presence floating on the wall. It is a good choice for unexpected places, like an open stairwell or a forgotten spot in a hall or entryway, as well as in more traditional placements like above a mantel, credenza, or sofa.

—

TIP Fresh willow branches are very elastic and can be bent into shape easily. Find them at your florist, or perhaps even in your backyard—use the straight, not curly, variety.

materials

24 flexible fresh willow branches,
  1 to 2 yd/1 to 2 m long

Spool of 24-gauge black wire

Wire cutters

Hammer and small nails

continued

ASSEMBLY

1 Divide the branches into eight bunches of three branches each. Arrange the bunches so that all the thicker ends of the branches face the same direction.

2 Secure the thicker ends of each bunch by wrapping a piece of the wire around them and twisting the ends together. Braid each bunch, starting at the thicker end and working your way to the thin end. Depending on how fresh or dry the branches are, sometimes the end of the braid will hold together on its own, and sometimes it won't. You can secure it with a piece of the wire if need be.

3 Take one pair of braids, and lay them together with the thicker ends pointing down. Take a second pair of braids and lay them together with the thicker ends pointing up. Overlap the thicker ends of both pairs of braid about a foot or so, and wire all of the thick ends together. You will end up with one long piece that tapers off at each end. To create a hanging loop, cut a 6-in/15-cm piece of wire, fold it in half, then twist it at the new halfway point to make a loop and two free ends. Wrap the two free ends around the point where the thick ends of the braids are wired together and twist to secure in place. Repeat this process with the remaining four braids, wiring them together and creating the hanging loop.

4 Hammer two nails into the wall about 4 ft/120 cm apart, and hang one completed braided willow piece vertically by its loop from each nail.

5 Once the two pieces are secured to the wall, bend the thin ends at the top toward each other and wire them together at a few points to connect them. Some of the branches can be left a bit loose and tucked behind one another to make an oval shape. Repeat with the thin ends at the bottom to complete the oval.

—

care

Some of the willow branches may need to be tucked back into the wreath occasionally, but no other maintenance is required.

16

IKEBANA INSPIRATION
IN COLOR

Ikebana is a Japanese art form hundreds of years old in which nature is controlled in a precise and minimalist style. Despite its long history, ikebana offers a contemporary way to display flowers in lieu of a traditional vase. This is a modern interpretation of the moribana style of ikebana, where a shallow container is used in conjunction with needle-style flower frogs to keep the stems upright. I like the shift in scale, how you can see more of the stem and the entire bloom with this approach. Play with shapes and textures—they don't all need to be flowers; you could also incorporate big leaves (such as the black cordyline in the back of this arrangement) or berried branches (like the tiny purple beautyberry).

materials

A selection of flower stems
  in a monochromatic palette
Low-rising vessel
Assorted flower frogs
Bucket of water
Garden shears

continued

TIP For this style of ikebana, any low-rising vessel will do; I found this copper dish (see page 125) at a flea market, but you may have something similar already in your home. Use a few different sizes of flower frogs so you can have some flexibility with your design. And you don't need heaps of flowers—you can make something chic and beautiful with only a few flowers or stems.

TIP Visit your local florist to gather a few select specimens in a monochromatic palette; I wanted an intense violet color so I used *Callicarpa americana* (beautyberry), purple anthurium, black wheat, *Scabiosa stellata* (starflower pincushions), *Gomphrena* (globe amaranth), and black cordyline here.

ASSEMBLY

1 Arranging the flowers will involve a bit of trial and error. Choose a central specimen or two (I like to start with the taller or wider pieces, then progress to the smaller, finer elements). Have the water-filled vessel and several flower frogs on hand as you prepare the flowers individually. Holding the stem end underwater in the bucket, make a fresh cut 1 to 2 in/2.5 to 5 cm up the stem. Then measure out each stem by eye against the flower frog inside the vessel, to determine the desired height. Clip off excess stem as needed to get the look you want, and insert immediately into the frog. Be mindful that the stem isn't so long it folds over; it should be able to stand upright on its own once secured onto the frog.

2 Once you've placed your center flower, fill in the arrangement with supporting stems, placing the stems in the same flower frog or adding additional frogs to play around with spacing. Each stem will need a fresh cut before it is placed in the frog. Experiment with high and low placements to make a graceful composition.

care

Add enough water to your container to cover the needles of the flower frogs to be sure your selections get enough water, and change the water daily. How long your arrangement will last depends on the types of flowers and stems you use. In general, branches and foliage tend to last longer than blooming flowers. Some flowers last only a few days; others can last a week or more. Keep your arrangement out of direct sunlight as heat can shorten its lifespan.

17

SUCCULENT
LANDSCAPE

This miniature arid landscape features the amazing starburst–like *Euphorbia mammillaris variegata*. I admire its unusual pale green, gray, and pinkish coloring, which is complemented by the stony gray–green of the *Echeveria lilacina* planted beneath it. The contrast in scale makes a striking composition. A low dish like this one frames the forms and highlights the subtle palette of gray tones.

—

TIP When working with prickly succulents, always wear gloves. Loosely wrapping the plants with paper towels will minimize the pricks as well as protect the delicate needles when re-potting them.

materials

Wide low bowl

Drainage stones

Activated horticultural carbon

Succulent potting soil

1 or 2 tall succulents about 10 in/
    25 cm in height

5 low-lying succulents each about 2 to
    3 in/5 to 7.5 cm in diameter

Sand, colored to complement bowl
    (available at garden supply centers)

continued

ASSEMBLY

1 Prepare the bowl for planting. First place a layer of drainage stones about 1 in/2.5 cm deep in the bottom, add a layer of horticultural carbon, then add your potting soil.

2 Start by planting the tall center plant or plants first. To re-pot, invert the plant and tap the rim of the pot to loosen the pot from the compost. If the plant is in a flexible plastic pot, squeezing the pot gently may help to loosen the root ball. It is better to break or cut the pot to free a compacted root ball than damage the plant. Remove the pot and clear away the old compost from the roots. Use your fingers to gently untangle the roots and remove old soil.

3 Add the low-lying succulents, encircling the tall plant. Place them in the soil so the top of the root ball is just at the surface and make sure they are stable.

4 Once everything is planted, fill in any necessary areas with potting soil.

5 Starting in the center and working outward toward the edges, slowly sprinkle a layer of sand on top of the potting soil to cover it.

—

care

Allow the plants to rest for about two weeks before watering to allow broken roots to recover. Succulents can withstand almost anything, and some have been known to last 20 years or more. A landscape like this need only be watered once a week in warmer months. When the weather is cooler many succulents rest, and, depending on temperature, humidity, and light levels, they may need less water so increase the time between each watering. Cacti and succulents can adapt to wide fluctuations of temperature. Exposure to temperatures between 40 and 90°F/4 and 32°C for long periods is not harmful. Let the potting mixture dry out between waterings and be very mindful not to overwater this style of dish planting—there are no drainage holes, so you only want to water enough to wet the soil but not have it soaking wet. When watering, first brush away an area in the sand very close to the plant, then carefully pour water from a small spouted vessel or through a small funnel so that it absorbs around the plant but does not wet the rest of the sand. Let it dry a bit, then brush or sprinkle the sand back into place. Use a small paintbrush to brush away any sand that nestles into the spines and crevices of the succulents.

FLOATING PRESSED BOTANICALS

Framed in black tape and frozen in time under glass, these arrangements of dried, pressed flowers and foliage are a two-dimensional reinterpretation of classic scientific specimen boxes. Clear panes of glass showcase even the most intricate of silhouettes, seemingly suspended in midair. A random placement of the materials takes on an organic composition, while a strategic placement is more graphic. I like to display the finished pieces by composing a variety of frame sizes and plants layered in a group so you can see dimensional effect through the layers of glass. Presented this way, they look like works of art atop a dresser or sideboard, but you could also place them on a shallow shelf or rail.

materials

Fresh-cut specimens for pressing or
    pre-pressed botanicals

Paper towels (if pressing flowers)

Blank newsprint paper (if pressing
    flowers; available at art supply stores)

Large heavy books, phone books
    suggested (if pressing flowers)

Lint-free cloth

Window cleaner

Pairs of glass panes (8½-by-11-in/
    22-by-28-cm, 12-by-16-in/30.5-by-
    41-cm, and 20-by-28-in/51-by-71-cm
    sizes used here)

Sobo craft glue

Brush for glue

1-in/2.5-cm gold-tone binder clips or
    ¾-in-/2-cm-wide black friction tape
    (available at hardware stores)

Scissors (if using tape)

Spoon (if using tape)

continued

TIP You can press flowers or interesting foliage yourself, or buy them ready-pressed. For this project, I used Queen Anne's lace, columbine flowers, dusty miller leaves, lace-leaf Japanese maple, and tree ferns.

TIP Get panes cut to size at a hardware store or window glazier, or repurpose pairs of panes from inexpensive glass clip frames. You can choose to hold the panes together with black friction tape to resemble framing or with binder clips for a more industrial effect.

ASSEMBLY

1 Press fresh-cut specimens yourself (or skip this step and use pre-pressed botanicals). Pick your flowers and leaves at their freshest and blot with paper towels to dry any moisture before pressing. Give some thought as to how the flower or foliage will look when flattened, then place the plants between two sheets of blank news-print paper and insert the sandwiched specimens into the pages of a heavy book. Choose a book large enough to press the botanicals and one where you will not be upset if the page possibly gets a little wet during the pressing—a telephone book is ideal. Separate the pressings by at least $1/8$ in/3 mm for best results. Weigh the book down with other heavy books and leave undisturbed a couple of weeks until the specimens have dried completely.

2 Use a lint-free cloth and window cleaner to clean glass panes on both sides before you begin your arrangement.

3 Select a pressed botanical to display. Create arrangements using multiples of a single plant type or a variety of plants in different frames to keep the look modern and create a graphic composition; mixed specimens in one frame can vary in thickness and might affect how the panes hold together. Analyze your dried specimens before making your final choice.

4 Position the specimens on one pane of glass as desired. Let the shape of the botanicals inspire you: experiment with random placement or more structured designs like a grid or wreath.

5 Once you have arranged the specimens, use a brush to apply a few very small dots of craft glue to secure the botanicals to one pane of glass. Let dry for about 2 hours.

6 Top with a second pane, then connect the two together with binder clips or friction tape. To use clips: Clip one binder clip at the top of the panes and one at the bottom. To use friction tape: Working on one side at a time, cut a piece to fit, adding about ¼ in/6 mm overlap at each corner. Center the tape on the edge of the panes and press into place over each side, folding the tape over itself at the corners. Use the back of a spoon to burnish the tape to adhere it completely and make a sharp finish around the edges.

—

care

Keep out of direct sunlight to minimize fading. Should you need to clean the glass once the project is finished, be careful not to get any moisture in between the panes of glass. If you have used friction tape to connect the panes, do not get the tape wet.

INDOOR
WATER GARDEN

This may be one of the simplest of projects in the book, but it is also one of the most striking. To create "the garden," I like to choose a variety of water plants and feature each individually in its own container. In this arrangement, water moss floats freely, while pennywort, vallis, and Amazon sword are anchored in beds of river stones.

—

TIP Most aquatic plants are sold with a small basket encasing their roots; keep it on. This helps to anchor the plant underneath a base of river stones. Completed water gardens are difficult to move, so do this project close to where you plan to display it.

materials

Tall clear glass containers

Aquatic plants

Black river stones

Filtered, unchlorinated water

continued

ASSEMBLY

1 Choose which container best suits each plant, and work one at a time. For example, taller plants will thrive in slender vertical shapes, while spreading plants such as pennywort will need a wider container.

2 Layer a few river stones into the bottom of the container for a base. Carefully remove the plant from any packaging and remove any yellowing or damaged leaves. Decide on positioning; once you have an arrangement that feels comfortable, add in more stones to cover up the root basket if there is one, and anchor the plant in place.

3 Start adding filtered, unchlorinated water slowly a little bit at a time so as not to disrupt the plants or the arrangement.

4 Continue adding water slowly until you reach about 2 in/5 cm from the top.

—

care

Because the water is standing and has no aeration, you'll need to replace it over the course of a week. Keep a bucket close by and scoop out about one-quarter of the water daily and replace it with fresh water. Adding liquid carbon and an aquatic plant fertilizer (available at aquarium supply stores) will keep the plants healthy. With good care, the plants should last several years. Avoid placing aquatic gardens in direct sunlight to limit the growth of algae; filtered sunlight is best. If you must move a container, remove some of the water and always pick it up from the bottom, not the top.

№ **20**

DRIED FLORAL
GARLAND

In my travels through India, I saw many incredible ceremonial garlands of fresh flowers, which inspired this everlasting project. At a luxurious 16 ft/5 m in length and with an abundance of nature's varieties, this garland is far from simple. It is a riot of color, a mad combination of shape and texture but confined into one fine line. Here it serves as a beautiful necklace on the wall, but you might also hang it over curtain hardware near a window. There's no particular pattern for this garland; feel free to experiment with limiting the lineup to two or three hues or types of flowers.

—

TIP For this garland, I purchased assorted inexpensive dried flowers in bulk and supplemented them with specific specimens like *Limonium* (statice), *Echinops ritro* (globe thistle), *Celosia* (cockscomb), *Delphinium* (larkspur), *Physalis* (Chinese lanterns), *Craspedia* (billy buttons), and wheat. Cutting the heads off of dried flowers yourself will give the most exacting results.

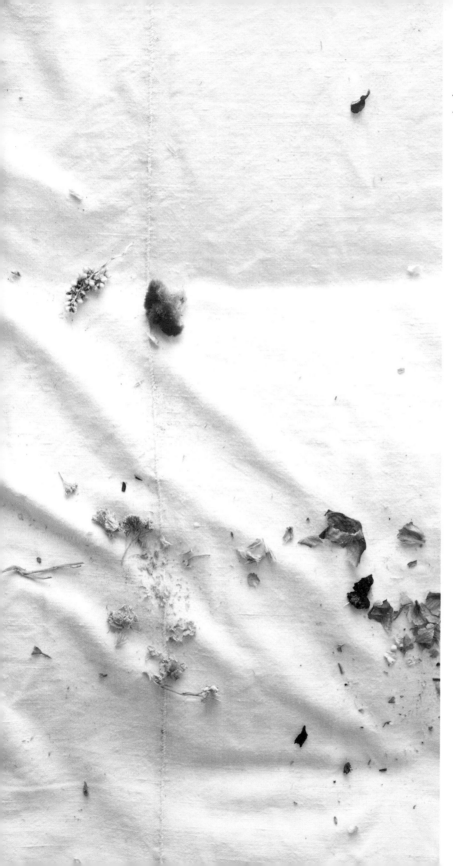

materials

Scissors

White polyester thread

Hand sewing needle

Approximately 1 lb/0.5 kg of dried
  flower heads, buds, and pods

Small nails (optional)

continued

ASSEMBLY

1 Cut a piece of thread the length of the garland you would like, plus a little extra; the garland here is 16 ft/5 m long.

2 Working on a large table or the floor, use the needle and thread and begin stringing dried elements until you reach the middle of the length of thread. Then, rethread the needle on the other end of the thread and begin again from the other direction so you are not pulling so much thread through each dried piece. If it's too laborious to thread the elements onto such a long piece of thread, try cutting it into three shorter lengths, threading them separately, then tying them together when completed. Some pieces may crumble a bit, but keep going; use leftover elements to fill in if need be (just wrap the bit of thread around the stem of a flower head or piece of wheat). If you have a piece that is too awkward to pierce properly, wrap the thread around a secure part of it and make a single knot to hold it and continue. Keep an eye on the composition as you go, spacing colors and shapes as you wish.

3 Once you have finished stringing, tie a knot at each end; you may need to double or triple the knot until it is thick enough to prevent any dried elements from slipping off, or use a plant at each end that you can readily create a loop around.

4 The garland is ready to hang. Be sure to move it very gently to prevent bits from breaking off. Drape it over the corner of a frame on a wall or hang it from a pair of small nails and let the ends fall gracefully to the floor.

—

care

Dried flowers are delicate, so be sure to hang your garland somewhere it will not be bumped a lot. It may fade in sunlight over time, but that's part of its romantic beauty.

single stem arrangement

Sometimes, one amazing stem is all you need to create an incredible arrangement. In this case, it is a single, massive stem of banksia, an exotic flower you can order fresh from your florist or buy pre-dried. With its saw-toothed foliage and prickly flower head, the prehistoric-looking banksia is a stunning object in itself that asks for little else in the way of embellishment. If you have been resistant to the idea of having dried flowers in your home, this ancient beauty may convince you. The fresh, spiky leaves will curl beautifully into muted shades of its original color as they dry; leaves of pre-dried banksias will need to be steamed a bit to get them to fall gracefully again. If you can't find banksias where you live, you could create a similar arrangement with a protea flower.

Select a vase. Banksias are top-heavy, so look for a vase that is tall enough to support the stem nearly up to the flower head with a base wide enough to prevent the vase from tipping over. Something with visual and physical weight is best for this project.

Then, prepare the banksia. The stems can be quite long; you may first need to trim off some of the stem and remove any bottom leaves so the flower will fit in the vase. To dry a freshly cut banksia for the best color and dramatically cascading foliage, simply place the flower upright in a vase (without water) in a dark, dry area for two to three weeks. Richer shades of the original, natural colors will better preserve in low light and low moisture conditions. Use a soft paintbrush for occasional dustings.

№ 21

DECONSTRUCTED
TOPIARY TRELLIS

Classic topiaries are often designed in rigid geometrical shapes such as globes or cones. I prefer a less formal approach, allowing the vines to grow a little free and wild on a deconstructed form. The effect is delicate rather than dense, but you'll still have tempered a wild-growing vine within the confines of your home.

—

TIP While any of a number of vines could be used for this project, angel ivy is one of my favorites for its very small, refined leaves. Choose a plant that is well branched and full. Alternatively, plant a couple of smaller ivy plants around the base; these individual plants can be trained up the frame in the same way and will eventually grow to look like one plant.

TIP A black terra-cotta pot has a more sophisticated look compared to conventional rust-colored versions and contrasts nicely with the green of the ivy leaves.

materials

Angel ivy, or other vine

10-in-/25-cm-diameter by 12-in-/
    30-cm-tall black terra-cotta pot

Potting soil

Garden shears

Twigs

Waxed twine

continued

ASSEMBLY

1 Repot your ivy or other vine in the pot, adding soil as needed.

2 Assemble the twig trellis frame. Cut one twig approximately 4 ft/120 cm long, and two or three others 12 to 14 in/30 to 36 cm long. Position the two shorter twigs horizontally about 6 in/15 cm apart on the main support; to attach them, wrap waxed twine crisscross around each point until it is secure, then tie a knot. Carefully insert the base of the finished twig frame into the center of the pot all the way to the bottom.

3 Let some of the vines at the base cascade over the sides of the pot, and train a few of the longer vines onto the frame. If the vines are a bit thick and unruly, trim and thin them out some-what to better reveal the individual vines and eliminate the bulk. Distribute the vines evenly, and gently twist the individual vines around the twigs of the frame. It may be necessary in the begin-ning to hold the vines in place with small ties of waxed twine. As the ivy grows, continue to train and twist the stems up the frame.

—

care

Place your topiary in bright or indirect light. Angel ivy is fast-growing—prune it regularly to maintain the shape you prefer. New growth can be trained onto the frame or snipped off. Every year or two the plant will probably need to be repot-ted. To do so, simply remove the plant from its pot with trellis intact, and gently loosen the root ball. Place the topiary in a container 1 to 2 in/2.5 to 5 cm larger, fill in with additional soil, and water thoroughly. Continue to train and trim the vine along the trellis.

FLOWER POCKET

In this update to the old May Day tradition of leaving baskets of flowers on a doorstep, a fabric flower pocket adds a temporary bright spot to a doorknob, a hook on the wall, or the bedpost. I've filled this pocket with poppies and anemones, but any cut flowers from your garden or florist will work (just avoid anything too top-heavy, which might cause the pocket to fall over). While these flowers have a casual "just-picked" look, the secret is that they are tucked into individual florists' water tubes to keep them fresh.

——

Finished size of Flower Pocket (not including ties): 7 by 18 in/18 by 46 cm

TIP I designed the pocket with rubber-coated linen fabric because I liked the raincoat-like feeling, but of course you could sew a pocket of any fabric you like. You'll find the pattern for sewing the pocket on page 165. Note that the linen has a coated side and an uncoated side; for this project the coated side will be referred to as the right side and the uncoated side will be the wrong side.

materials

Pocket Back and Pocket Template
  (see page 165)
Fabric scissors
⅝ yd/0.6 m of rubber-coated linen
  (at least 52 in/132 cm wide)
Straight pins
Polyester thread
Sewing machine
Individual florist's water tube for
  each stem
Fresh cut flowers
Bucket of water
Garden shears

continued

ASSEMBLY

1 Photocopy the pattern on the facing page enlarging by 400 percent.

2 Cut the Pocket patterns and pin to fabric. Cut two Pocket Back pieces and one Pocket piece from fabric. Cut one long rectangular piece (2 by 52 in/5 by 132 cm) for the Tie.

3 Hem the Pocket piece. With the Pocket piece wrong side up, fold the straight 8-in/20-cm edge ½ in/1.5 cm, wrong sides together. Pin folded edge in place and sew a straight stitch with a ½-in/1.5-cm seam allowance ⅜ in/1 cm from folded edge, to make a hem. Back stitch at the beginning and end of stitching. Stitch ¼ in/0.5 cm from the edge.

4 Layer the pieces into a sandwich aligning the rounded edges. Place one of the Pocket Back pieces flat with the right side up. Then place the Pocket piece on top of the Pocket Back piece, with right side up, aligning along the rounded edges. Finally, place the second Pocket Back piece on top of Pocket piece, with wrong side up, aligning along the rounded edges. The Pocket piece will be sandwiched between the two Pocket Back pieces; pin the pieces together to hold them in place.

5 Leave the straight top edge open. Start at one of the top corners and sew the three other edges of the pocket together with a ½-in/1.5-cm seam allowance. Clip the seam allowances to avoid puckering. Remove pins and turn right side out through the opening, so the Pocket is exposed.

6 Prepare the Tie piece. With Tie fabric uncoated side up, fold over each long edge of the fabric ½ in/1.5 cm toward the center, wrong sides together, then fold the entire piece in half lengthwise so the two opposite folded edges meet and the Tie piece measures ½ by 52 in/1.5 by 132 cm. Pin folded edges together.

continued

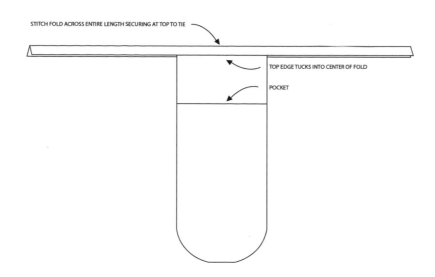

STITCH FOLD ACROSS ENTIRE LENGTH SECURING AT TOP TO TIE

TOP EDGE TUCKS INTO CENTER OF FOLD

POCKET

POCKET
cut 1

POCKET BACK
cut 2

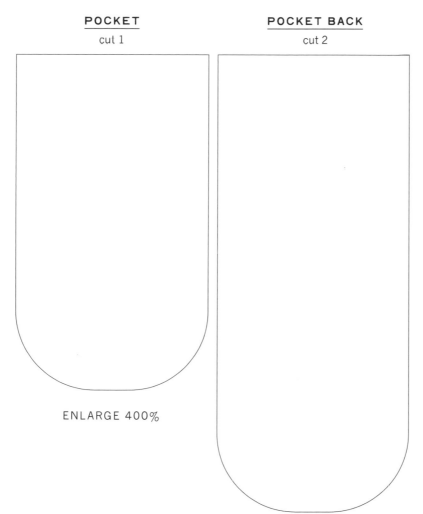

ENLARGE 400%

7 Attach Tie to Pocket Back. With pinned Tie piece lying flat, center the completed Pocket Back along the length of the Tie. The Pocket Back will be placed approximately 22½ in/57 cm in from each end of the Tie. Remove any pins from the center of the Tie piece that are in the way and insert the unsewn top edge of the Pocket Back between the folded edges of the Tie (the top edge of the Pocket Back will be sandwiched between the folded edges of the tie). Pin Pocket Back in place. Sew along the entire length of the two folded edges of the Tie, ⅛ in/0.3 cm from the folded edge, catching the Pocket Back in this seam. Leave the ends of the Tie unsewn.

8 Knot both ends of the Tie together to form a loop.

9 Fill the individual florist's tubes with water.

10 Prepare the flowers individually. Holding the stem end underwater in the bucket, make a fresh cut 1 to 2 in/2.5 to 5 cm up the stem, then immediately insert the stem end into a water tube.

11 Arrange the flowers into the Pocket and hang from a doorknob or hook.

—

care

Change the water in the tubes every other day, making a fresh cut on each stem end. How long your arrangement will last depends on the types of flowers you use and the heat and humidity in your home. Hanging the pocket in direct sunlight will decrease the lifespan of the flowers. The pocket and the tubes can be reused (be sure to wash out the tubes well).

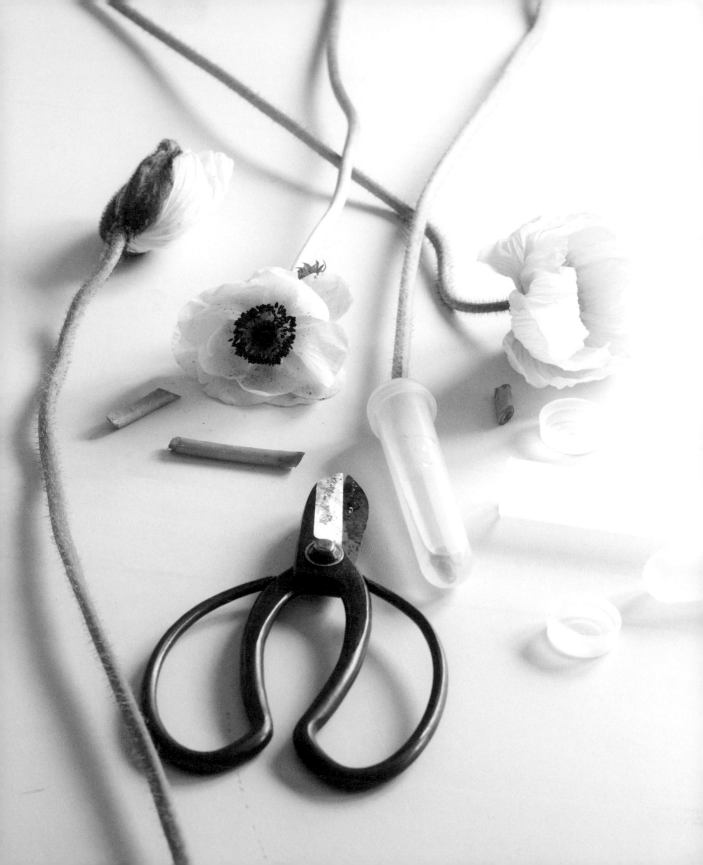

SOURCES

I believe good supplies can be found in many different places, and have always looked beyond traditional garden centers to find some of the more interesting objects and plant specimens. I've collected some of my favorite sources here to make it easier for you to find what you need to recreate the projects in this book. Of course, live goods are always variable and stocks of supplies can change, so be open to experimentation with other colors, finishes, and materials. Your best source may be your own home—look around to see what you may already have that can be adapted to the projects. Vintage shops and flea markets are also great resources for all sorts of vessels, and these one-of-a-kind items can ultimately help make the project feel more personal.

CRAFT & FLORIST SUPPLIES In this section you'll find where to buy specific planting materials and supplies, tools, and crafting essentials as used in these projects.

Activated horticultural carbon
www.aquariumguys.com
www.petco.com

Aquatic plant fertilizer
www.seachem.com

Art boards
www.art-boards.com

Black river stones
www.jamaligarden.com

Blank newsprint paper
www.dickblick.com

Bonsai shears
www.jamaligarden.com

Colored sand
www.jamaligarden.com

Crystals
www.exquisitecrystals.com

Custom vitrine
www.museumboxes.com

FloraCraft StyroGlue
www.joann.com

Flower frogs
www.jamaligarden.com

Garden shears
www.jamaligarden.com

Gilding supplies
www.dickblick.com

Glass clip frames
www.aifriedman.com
www.amazon.com

Glass crystals
www.jamaligarden.com

Individual florist's water tubes
www.save-on-crafts.com

Jute twine
www.jamaligarden.com

Manila rope
www.jamaligarden.com

Oasis Sahara Dry Floral Foam
www.jamaligarden.com

Paving stones
www.lowes.com

Rubber-coated linen
www.bandjfabrics.com

Sobo Craft Glue
www.dickblick.com

Spherical paper lanterns
www.pearlriver.com

Waxed linen twine
www.bellomodo.com

DRIED & LIVE PLANT MATERIALS
Some favorite suppliers of dried flowers and plants, as well as categories such as aquatic plants, succulents, ferns, *Tillandsia*, and more.

Aquatic plants

www.aquariumplants.com

www.aquariumplantsandsupplies.com

www.azgardens.com

All three of these sources offer an amazing selection as well as a wealth of information on aquatic plant care.

Banksias

www.proteas.com

Dried flowers

www.driedflowersdirect.com

Offers a good variety of dried flowers, but the offerings are seasonal and may not be carried all year-round

Dry Nature

245 W 29th St #1

New York, NY 10001

212.695.4104

A small shop in New York's flower district that supplies fine examples of dried botanicals; call for special requests and to order

www.nettletonhollow.com

Specializes in high-quality decorative branches and lasting botanicals

Ferns

www.forestfarm.com

A good range of ferns and a large selection of plants available to ship

Ivy

Hedera, Etc., Russell A. Windle

P.O. Box 461

Lionville, PA 19353

610.970.9175 | hedera@att.net

Lichens

www.sprouthome.com

Specializes in indoor gardening accessories in small quantities

Moss

www.mossacres.com

A good resource for live mosses; the site also offers wonderful growing tips and useful information.

Natural hollow tree stumps

www.save-on-crafts.com

Pressed flowers and botanicals

www.naturespressed.com

A great selection of hand-pressed flowers and botanicals in a variety of quantities

Succulents

www.simplysucculents.com

An inspiring and unusual range of succulents

Tillandsia

www.airplantshop.com

Small selection of *Tillandsias* and care info

www.airplantsupplyco.com

A well-edited selection of *Tillandsia* varieties and accessories

Willow branches

www.nettletonhollow.com

POTS, PLANTERS & VESSELS Many of these sources
stock more than just pots, and also provide visual inspiration for designing your
own projects.

www.anchorhocking.com
A classic American company that makes
heavy-wearing glassware that can be
reimagined into terrariums and other
floral vessels

www.floragrubb.com
Stocks a forward-thinking and stylish range
of handmade and industrial garden products

www.grdnbklyn.com
A Brooklyn shop offering classic pots and
garden accessories that blend well into
modern or traditional homes

www.jamaligarden.com
This New York City flower district shop car-
ries the soup to nuts of garden supplies
available to trade and to the public; some
supplies are available in bulk.

www.save-on-crafts.com
A vast assortment of raw craft and decorative items, with a range of natural products
as well as glass vessels in many shapes
and sizes

www.shopterrain.com
A garden wonderland outside of Philadelphia
filled with unusual outdoor and indoor plants;
they also sell an aesthetically pleasing range
of home accessories and garden products.

www.sprouthome.com
This Brooklyn garden shop caters to the
urban (or any indoor) gardener, with small-
scale pots, accessories, and plenty of
indoor plants.

www.westelm.com
In addition to my own collection, this modern
home furnishings retailer offers a beautiful
assortment of indoor garden vessels for cut
flower arrangements and indoor terrariums.

SUGGESTED READING Here is a small collection of books that I refer to again and again for inspiration in my work. Out-of-print books can be found at flea markets and on websites such as www.abe.com or www.alibris.com.

The Art of Arranging Flowers: A Complete Guide to Japanese Ikebana
by Shozo Sato
Tuttle Publishing 1965 (reissued 2008)
A giant tome of flower arranging with beautiful images and clear instructions. The inspiration in this book goes beyond ikebana alone.

Bloom: Horticulture for the 21st Century
by Li Edelkoort
Flammarion 2001
With lush photography and styling, this visionary book illustrates abstract and emotional connections between man and nature.

Botany for Gardeners, Third Edition
by Brian Capon
Timber Press 2010
A highly accessible and clear introduction to the science of plants

Ocean Flowers: Impressions from Nature
by Carol Armstrong and Catherine de Zegher
Princeton University Press 2004
A stunning beauty on natural history imagery in the mid-nineteenth century, with particular emphasis on botanical drawings and photograms

The Pictorial Encyclopedia of Plants and Flowers
by F.A. Novak
Outlet 1966
An amazing visual feast of plant and flower photography with good information

The Pressed Plant
by Andrea DiNoto and David Winter
Abrams 1999
This is a beautifully illustrated book examining the art of preserving nature.

INDEX

ACKNOWLEDGMENTS

This book would not have been possible without the collaboration of many generous and talented people.

Thank you Jodi Warshaw, Laura Lee Mattingly, and Lisa Tauber at Chronicle Books for granting me this very privileged opportunity. Thank you, too, for your respect toward the ever-evolving creative process.

Thanks also to:
Photographers Andrea Gentl and Martin Hyers; it is without question that every idea and detail was illuminated through your lens with loving care. Your effortless style and fine craftsmanship is evident in every spot of ink throughout these pages. Big heart also to Meredith Munn for keeping all of us organized and making sure things were in focus and filed correctly.

Jennifer Cegielski for your keen attention to the intent, process, and words that appear in this book. Thank you for following my tracks so generously and with a sense of humor.

My dramaturge, Addys Gonzalez, for your everlasting patience, critical eye, and stunt-level driving skills that took us all over upstate New York and beyond in a giant 1983 Mercedes-Benz stuffed with pots, plants, twigs, stones, dirt, and buckets of fresh cut flowers.

An enormous hug to all who opened their beautiful homes for the image creation in this book (and gave shelter while we were shooting) . . . Andrea Gentl and Martin Hyers, Anne Johnson, Chad Jacobs and Stephen Orr, Corinne Gilbert, Lisa Ilario and John Philp. It is the heart and soul of your homes that brought these ideas to life.

Thank you also to Marcie McGoldrick for your generous heart and mind, Stephanie Hung for your amazingly refined crafting skills, Alberto Capolino for your muscles and thoughtful cooking while on location, and Philip Fimmano for flawless insight.

Finally to my mother and father who never gave me a curfew, overlooked my poor performance in mathematics, and allowed my imagination to wander wild and free.